ideals® SUMMERTIME

Now Summer waves her magic wand
And casts a spell of languid days
On peaceful hills, on rocky shores,
On sparkling, sheltered little bays.
She blesses with her smiling skies
A bright vacation paradise.

Brian F. King

ISBN 0-8249-1062-1

Publisher, Patricia A. Pingry
Editor, Peggy Schaefer
Art Director, Patrick McRae
Production Manager, Jan Johnson
Editorial Assistant, Kathleen Gilbert
Copy Editor, Joan Anderson

IDEALS—Vol. 45, No. 4 June MCMLXXXVIII IDEALS (ISSN 0019-137X) is published eight times a year,
February, March, May, June, August, September, November, December
by IDEALS PUBLISHING CORPORATION, Nelson Place at Elm Hill Pike, Nashville, Tenn. 37214
Second class postage paid at Nashville, Tennessee, and additional mailing offices.
Copyright © MCMLXXXVIII by IDEALS PUBLISHING CORPORATION.
POSTMASTER: Send address changes to Ideals, Post Office Box 148000, Nashville, Tenn. 37214-8000
All rights reserved. Title IDEALS registered U.S. Patent Office.

SINGLE ISSUE—$3.95
ONE-YEAR SUBSCRIPTION—eight consecutive issues as published—$17.95
TWO-YEAR SUBSCRIPTION—sixteen consecutive issues as published—$31.95
Outside U.S.A., add $6.00 per subscription year for postage and handling.

Front and back covers by Jeff Gnass

Inside front cover by Fred Sieb
Inside back cover from FPG International

Heart of the Year

Ida Scott Taylor

Out in the meadow the clover is growing,
Out in the sunshine the breezes are blowing,
Clover and breezes are dancing in glee,
Nodding and bowing their brightest to me;
This is the time when the birds are the fleetest,
This is the time when their songs are the sweetest,
This is the time when their notes are most clear,
Heart of the June time is heart of the year!

Now when the May trees are done with their blooming,
Now when the roses the air are perfuming,
Now when the lilies are turning to snow,
Nestling their soft creamy throats in a row,
Now is the time when the tongue wakes to gladness,
Breaking in song, as the brooks rush to madness,
Now is the time that we welcome most dear,
Heart of the June time is heart of the year!

Lifted above us the heavens are shining,
Azure and white, with a silvery lining,
Glories are there that our eyes cannot reach,
Things that are hidden from sight and from speech;
Heaven is o'er us about and above,
God is the Author and Father of Love;
God is within us, His spirit is near,
God in the June time is Heart of the Year!

Photo Opposite
QUEEN ELIZABETH PARK
VANCOUVER, BRITISH COLUMBI.
Thomas Kitchin
Tom Stack & Associates

Photo Overleaf
SAWYER HARBOR
Ken Dequaine

Flowers

Henry Wadsworth Longfellow

Spake full well, in language quaint and olden,
　One who dwelleth by the castled Rhine,
When he called the flowers, so blue and golden,
　Stars, that in earth's firmament do shine.

Stars they are, wherein we read our history,
　As astrologers and seers of old;
Yet not wrapped about with awful mystery,
　Like the burning stars, which they beheld.

Wondrous truths, and manifold as wondrous,
　God hath written in those stars above;
But not less in the bright flowerets under us
　Stands the revelation of his love.

Bright and glorious is that revelation,
　Written all over this great world of ours;
Making evident our own creation,
　In these stars of earth—these golden flowers.

And the Poet, faithful and farseeing,
　Sees, alike in stars and flowers, a part
Of the selfsame, universal being,
　Which is throbbing in his brain and heart.

Gorgeous flowerets in the sunlight shining,
　Blossoms flaunting in the eye of day,
Tremulous leaves, with soft and silver lining,
　Buds that open only to decay;

Brilliant hopes, all woven in gorgeous tissues,
　Flaunting gayly in the golden light;
Large desires, with most uncertain issues,
　Tender wishes, blossoming at night!

Summertime's Reign

Virginia K. Oliver

When summertime has come to reign,
  All nature seems to understand
That competition of the best
  Is taking place throughout the land.

The birds sing out their sweetest tunes,
  The trees and grass parade their green,
Flowers lift their faces up
  So their perfection may be seen.

The sun shines down the brightest rays,
  Then in the dark night way up high,
Stars appear like clustered jewels
  Twinkling in a royal sky.

As summer's pageantry unfolds,
  No single beauty excells the rest;
It takes them all together to
  Display this grand world at its best.

BRANFF NATIONAL PARK
ALBERTA, CANADA
Gene Ahrens

Woodland Glade

Edith Helstern

I wonder if the little wood
   That nestled into groves
Still has the tangled little paths
   That leave the old main road.

They stretched half-hidden through the brush
   And alders by the way,
And each path held a mystery
   That led my feet to stray.

Through turns and twists and out of sight,
   Shadows led me on
Along the path adventure-filled
   With shifting, whispered sound.

Magic seemed to flicker through
   The deep, green mossy shade,
And romance stole on tiptoe in
   The little wooded glade.

If I could leave the city lights
   And travel there again,
I'd find the little wooded paths
   And my childhood's fairyland.

Photo Opposite
MORAN STATE PARK
ORCAS ISLAND, WASHINGTON
Gene Ahrens

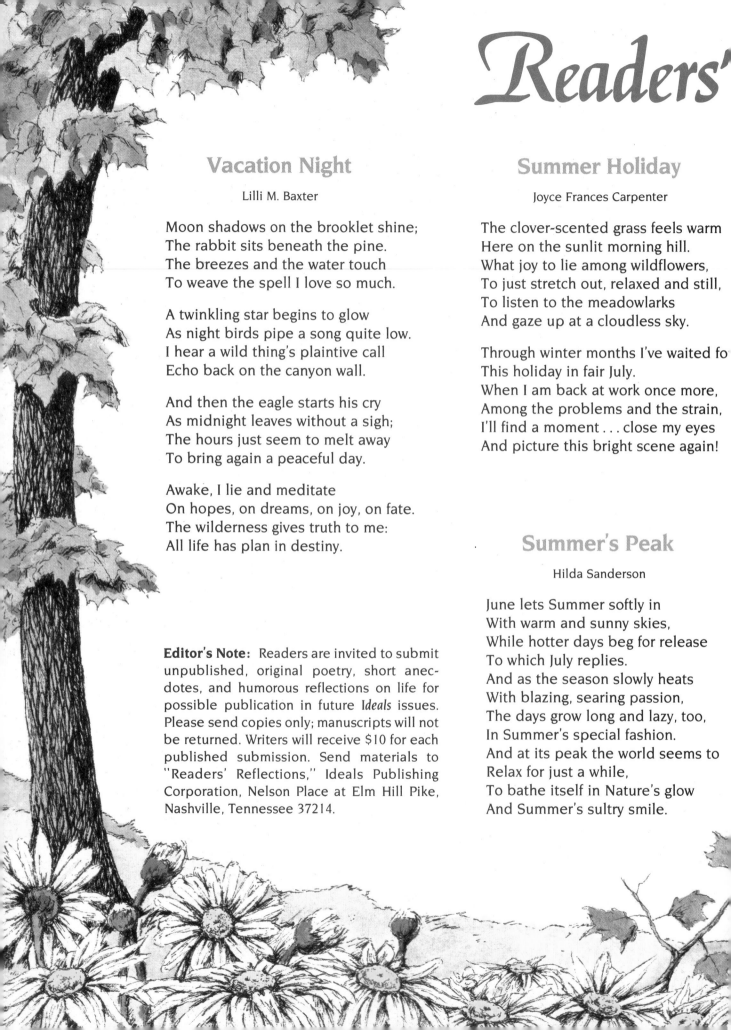

Vacation Night

Lilli M. Baxter

Moon shadows on the brooklet shine;
The rabbit sits beneath the pine.
The breezes and the water touch
To weave the spell I love so much.

A twinkling star begins to glow
As night birds pipe a song quite low.
I hear a wild thing's plaintive call
Echo back on the canyon wall.

And then the eagle starts his cry
As midnight leaves without a sigh;
The hours just seem to melt away
To bring again a peaceful day.

Awake, I lie and meditate
On hopes, on dreams, on joy, on fate.
The wilderness gives truth to me:
All life has plan in destiny.

Editor's Note: Readers are invited to submit unpublished, original poetry, short anecdotes, and humorous reflections on life for possible publication in future *Ideals* issues. Please send copies only; manuscripts will not be returned. Writers will receive $10 for each published submission. Send materials to "Readers' Reflections," Ideals Publishing Corporation, Nelson Place at Elm Hill Pike, Nashville, Tennessee 37214.

Summer Holiday

Joyce Frances Carpenter

The clover-scented grass feels warm
Here on the sunlit morning hill.
What joy to lie among wildflowers,
To just stretch out, relaxed and still,
To listen to the meadowlarks
And gaze up at a cloudless sky.

Through winter months I've waited fo
This holiday in fair July.
When I am back at work once more,
Among the problems and the strain,
I'll find a moment . . . close my eyes
And picture this bright scene again!

Summer's Peak

Hilda Sanderson

June lets Summer softly in
With warm and sunny skies,
While hotter days beg for release
To which July replies.
And as the season slowly heats
With blazing, searing passion,
The days grow long and lazy, too,
In Summer's special fashion.
And at its peak the world seems to
Relax for just a while,
To bathe itself in Nature's glow
And Summer's sultry smile.

Reflections

Hot-Air Balloons on Parade

Claire Hupe Burnham

I saw them rise,
One by one,
Like soap bubbles blown from pipes of
    clay,
Up from hidden launching pads
At the end of a sleepy summer's day.

Straight up they rose,
And higher yet,
Until they caught a vagrant breeze
That set them floating across the sky
Like sailing ships on sunlit seas.

I counted eight—
No, there were ten—
In the early evening's waning light,
Multicolored patchwork balloons
Adrift in magical, gala flight.

And my spirit lifted
With all the spheres
In the seemingly carefree, buoyant air.
Oh, what a delight to see them paint
The wandering sky with festive flair.

As the sinking sun
Gave signal to all
That night would soon enough descend,
They left the skies to light in fields,
Bringing the pageant to reluctant end.

I remember them moving
With weightless joy,
I see them, now, as they soar and play
Up where gentle winds have carried
    them—
Dipping, then lifting, still higher, and
    away.

Sunrise from Above

Grace Scott Pendlebury

I saw the world a spectacular way,
As God created a newborn day
From a frightening, rainy, turbulent night
Spent on a storm-tossed plane in flight.
As I entered a sky that was breaking
    clear,
God's voice was whispering, "Lo! I am
    here.
Be calm, and believe that life is long,
For you have proven your faith is strong."

I was calm . . . and beheld a holy sight:
As the sun broke through in a rose-hued
    light,
The clouds below us were billowing high,
Their edges lace-ruffled with rose from
    the sky.
Like waves of the ocean they'd appear,
Only whitecaps were rose caps floating
    near.
This was a new world of revealing grace,
A world where I saw, and touched, God's
    face.

Grand Canyon

Sharon Thompson-Dalegowski

Light tumbles through the canyon, illuminating,
  enhancing the depth and magnitude,
    no wonder they call it GRAND.

Ribbons of rock reflect rugged rainbows of color
  as the sun shoots rays of light
    over this magical land.

Ravens call, then tempt cliff walls,
  soaring and gliding, diving and riding,
    a squeaking and squawking band.

As we slip inside this rock riptide
  we are engulfed by color and canyon,
    mesa tops barely tanned.

We snake our way down from the pine-crested crown,
  rock towers to one side, walk or ride
    into the palm of the hand.

What a wonderful sight, nature's delight,
  with a spectrum of color before us,
    kaleidoscope of canyon fanned.

The bottom calls: amid the rock halls,
  nestled among the trees,
    lies comfort, the "Phantom" brand.*

*The identifying brand of the ranch at the bottom of the South Rim of the Grand
Canyon; it offers refreshments and other amenities to canyon visitors in agreement with
the Grand Canyon National Park Lodges.

Daddy's Girl

Garnett Ann Schultz

She's just a darling little girl, as precious as a lamb,
She rules our home in many ways that not another can.
She's in and out, and here and there, throughout our busy day,
And many times I stop my work because she wants to play.

She often has a special hug, the sweetest baby kiss,
And when just she and I are there, I get her treasured bliss;
But when her dad arrives at night, you'll find her in a whirl,
She hasn't time for Mother then, because she's Daddy's girl.

It's joy to see her laughing eyes, her happy baby smile,
'Tis then I know that all is well, and life is worth the while.
So lovingly he'll pinch her nose, or try to steal a curl,
Just anything he does is right, because she's Daddy's girl.

I often marvel at the charms that only dads possess,
Although I know within my heart she doesn't love me less.
We tuck her into bed at night, our one and only pearl,
And 'cause I love her daddy, too, I'm proud she's Daddy's girl.

Photo Opposite
FATHER'S LOVE
Murphy/Stills
H. Armstrong Roberts, Inc.

The Perfect Pair

Kathleen Y. Bergeron

Although they are different
As any you'd find,
They're bonded together,
Their lives intertwined.

Our daughter is fair-haired,
With eyes that are blue;
Her daddy is green-eyed,
His hair a dark hue.

My husband is strong, and
Yet when she is near,
His gentle side shows through
To her very clear.

For to our small daughter,
No special surprise
Could ever be better
Than Dad in her eyes.

If ever the Lord made
His love manifest,
It's here, for they both bring
Out each other's best.

A Father to His Son

Craig Sathoff

To stroll through woods with you, my son,
Upon a summer's night—
To hear the croon of nesting birds,
Just makes the day seem right.

The fishing trips, the rounds of chess,
The two-man games of ball,
Have brought a fine companionship
With faith and trust through all.

The wonderment that you possess,
I, too, have learned to share—
To thrill to rocks and sparkling stones,
To treat all life with care.

Though summer's sun may burn on high,
Or fields be white with fleece,
The friendship that we share, my son,
Has brought me joy and peace.

Photo Opposite
ORTH UMPQUA RIVER, OREGON
Ray Atkeson

When Father Was a Boy

Anonymous

The world was full of wondrous things
    When Father was a boy;
It almost seems like folks had wings
    When Father was a boy.
They liked to work the livelong day,
    And rise at five, and never play;
They just seemed to be built that way
    When Father was a boy.

The little boys were awfully strong
    When Father was a boy.
They'd weed the cornfields all day long
    When Father was a boy.
And when the day at last was o'er
    They'd go and do up every chore,
Then come and beg to work some more
    When Father was a boy.

The youngsters never had much fun
   When Father was a boy.
They'd go to bed when work was done
   When Father was a boy.
They only had a book or two,
   The clothes they wore were never new;
And, wow! The lessons they got through
   When Father was a boy!

The snow was thirty-two feet deep
   When Father was a boy;
They tunneled through to feed the sheep
   When Father was a boy.
The crust would freeze, and then they'd go
   And coast to town upon the snow
Without a stop, ten miles or so,
   When Father was a boy.

Young folks were seen and never heard
   When Father was a boy;
They couldn't say a single word
   When Father was a boy.
But now Dad loves to whoop and shout;
   I guess we kids have heard about
'Most all the talk he went without
   When Father was a boy.

Barbecue Apron

Ann Marie Braaten

Materials Needed:
1¼ yards medium-weight poplin
Broadcloth scraps—gray, terra cotta, green, red, tan

⅛ yard fusible interfacing
Matching thread

apron

cut one on fold

ties

cut four

pocket

cut one on fold

selvages

one square equals one inch

Directions:

Step One: Cutting Apron Pieces

Fold the 1¼ yards of apron fabric with selvages together.

Position and cut apron and pocket pieces on the fold.

Cut four 3 x 30-inch pieces for ties.

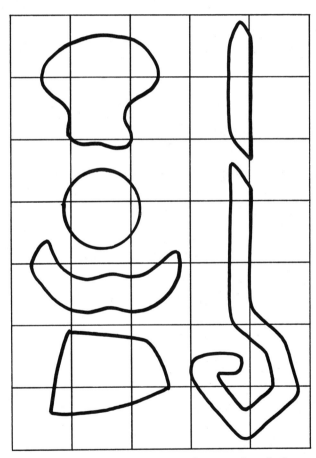

Cut two of each shape

Step Two: Preparing Appliqués

Press interfacing to the wrong side of the broadcloth scraps.

Cut shapes using appliqué patterns.

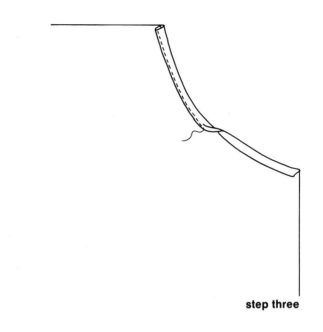

Step Three: Sewing Apron

Along the curved edges of the apron, press under ¼ inch twice.

Machine stitch the folded hem.

At the top of the apron press under ¼ inch. Press under again 1 inch. Stitch along the folded hem.

step three

Step Four: Attaching the Pocket

At top of pocket, press under ¼ inch. Press under again 1 inch. Stitch along folded hem.

Pin the right side of the pocket to the wrong side of apron with bottom and side edges even. Stitch a ½-inch seam along the bottom edge. Press pocket to right side.

Baste the pocket to the apron at the side edges. Hem each side by pressing under ¼ inch twice and stitching the fold.

To form the 3 pocket compartments, sew a seam vertically 9¾ inches from each side. Sew a bar tack at the top of each seam to reinforce seam strength.

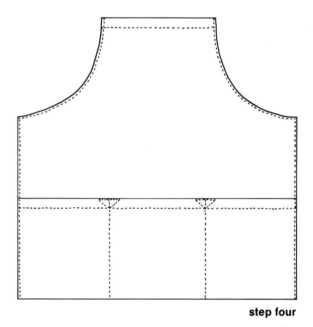

step four

Step Five: Attaching the Ties

Make the ties by folding each 3 x 30-inch strip in half lengthwise. Stitch a ⅜″ seam along one end and the entire length. With the remaining open end, turn the tie to the right side. Press.

Attach each tie to apron by pressing under the open end 1 inch and sewing the folded edge securely to the back side of apron at sides and front. Tack seam to reinforce seam strength.

Step Six: Appliquéing

Use a yardstick as a guide to position the 2 shish kebabs diagonally across the front of the apron. Pin each piece securely to the apron.

Using an appliqué or zigzag stitch (a fine stitch length with a medium zigzag works best), appliqué the skewers first. Then appliqué each meat shape, followed by the green peppers, tomatoes, and mushrooms.

Summertime Barbecue Kebabs

Makes 6 servings

Use your imagination and design your own kebabs! Skewer a selection of meat, poultry, fish, and vegetables. Marinate, if desired; grill or broil. Serve over rice with sauces.

Vegetables and Fruit

1 large onion, cut into chunks
1 large green *or* red pepper, cut into squares
10 to 12 large mushrooms
8 to 10 cherry tomatoes
6 to 8 ears frozen baby corn
8 to 10 cubes eggplant *or* zucchini *or* crookneck squash
8 small white onions
8 pineapple chunks

Meat, Poultry, and Fish

2 pounds cubed lamb (leg *or* shoulder roast) *or* cubed beef top round *or* cubed chicken *or* turkey breast
1½ pounds medium shrimp
1½ pounds thick fish fillets, cut into chunks

Marinades

Mediterranean Marinade
Indian Yogurt Marinade

Sauces

Sweet and Sour Sauce

Mediterranean Marinade

¼ cup olive oil
¼ cup lemon juice
¼ cup water
2 to 3 cloves garlic, minced

1 teaspoon basil leaves
½ teaspoon salt
¼ teaspoon ground coriander
¼ teaspoon freshly ground pepper

Blend all ingredients. Pour marinade over prepared kebabs. Marinate for 1 hour 30 minutes, turning once. Drain marinade from kebabs. Grill as desired.

Indian Yogurt Marinade

1 cup plain yogurt
1 small red onion, chopped
2 cloves garlic, minced
1 tablespoon minced crystallized ginger
1½ teaspoons ground cumin
1 teaspoon nutmeg

1 teaspoon chili powder
½ teaspoon cinnamon
½ teaspoon freshly ground pepper
¼ teaspoon ground cloves
¼ teaspoon ground cardamom

Combine all ingredients. Marinate for 1 hour 30 minutes, turning once. Drain marinade from kebabs. Grill as desired.

Sweet and Sour Sauce

8 ounces fresh *or* canned pineapple, pureed
1 tablespoon soy sauce
1 tablespoon brown sugar
1 tablespoon vinegar

1 to 2 cloves garlic, minced *or* pressed
¼ teaspoon ground ginger
1 tablespoon cornstarch
1 tablespoon water

In a small saucepan, combine pineapple puree, soy sauce, brown sugar, vinegar, garlic, and ginger. Bring to a boil; reduce heat. Simmer for 10 minutes. Dissolve cornstarch in water. Stir into sauce. Cook, stirring constantly, until sauce thickens.

The Path That Leads to Nowhere

Corinne Roosevelt Robinson

There's a path that leads to Nowhere
  In a meadow that I know,
Where an inland river rises
  And the stream is still and slow;
There it wanders under willows
  And beneath the silver green
Of the birches' silent shadows
  Where the early violets lean.

Other pathways lead to Somewhere,
  But the one I love so well
Has no end and no beginning—
  Just the beauty of the dell,
Just the windflowers and the lilies
  Yellow striped as adder's tongue,
Seem to satisfy my pathway
  As it winds their sweets among.

There I go to meet the Springtime,
  When the meadow is aglow,
Marigolds amid the marshes,
  And the stream is still and slow;
There I find my fair oasis,
  And with carefree feet I tread
For the pathway leads to Nowhere,
  And the blue is overhead.

All the ways that lead to Somewhere
  Echo with the hurrying feet
Of the Struggling and the Striving,
  But the way I find so sweet
Bids me dream and bids me linger—
  Joy and beauty are its goal;
On the path that leads to Nowhere
  I have sometimes found my soul.

Photo Opposite
MACKINAC ISLAND
ST. IGNACE, MICHIGAN
Ken Dequaine

Sounds of Freedom

Esther Bowman

Away out in the forest where
   There's peace and solitude,
I like to wander for awhile
   To freshen up my mood,
Forgetting tasks and deadlines of
   The frantic human race,
Adjusting all my steps to match
   Nature's gentler pace.

When I am hushed and still, I hear
   A multitude of sounds
That murmur in the forest deep
   Where vital life abounds:
The hum of busy insects by
   The gurgling of the brook,
The whisper of a playful breeze
   Exploring every nook,

The pattering of tiny feet
   Upon some mission brave,
The mournful sighing of the trees
   Whose mighty branches wave,
The oft repeated carols of
   The songsters of the air
Who sing and call and whistle as
   They seek their daily fare,

And now and then a crackling sound
   As something larger moves
Throughout the fallen leaves and twigs
   On padded feet or hooves.
These peaceful sounds are quite unlike
   The bustle, noise, and din,
The constant clamor of the times
   That we are living in.

And that is why I like to find
   From cares a sweet release
Out in the woods and countryside
   With nature's healing peace.

They Called It America

Rabbi Abba Hillel Silver

God built him a continent of glory, and filled it with treasures untold. He studded it with sweet-flowing fountains, and traced it with long-winding streams. He carpeted it with soft-rolling prairies, and columned it with thundering mountains. He graced it with deep-shadowed forests, and filled them with song.

Then he called unto a thousand peoples, and summoned the bravest among them. They came from the ends of the earth, each bearing a gift and a hope. The glow of adventure was in their eyes, and in their hearts the glory of hope.

And out of the bounty of earth, and the labor of men; out of the longing of heart and the prayer of souls; out of the memory of ages and the hopes of the world, God fashioned a nation in love, and blessed it with purpose sublime.

And they called it America.

Photo Opposite
BALD EAGLE
D & P Valenti
H. Armstrong Roberts, Inc

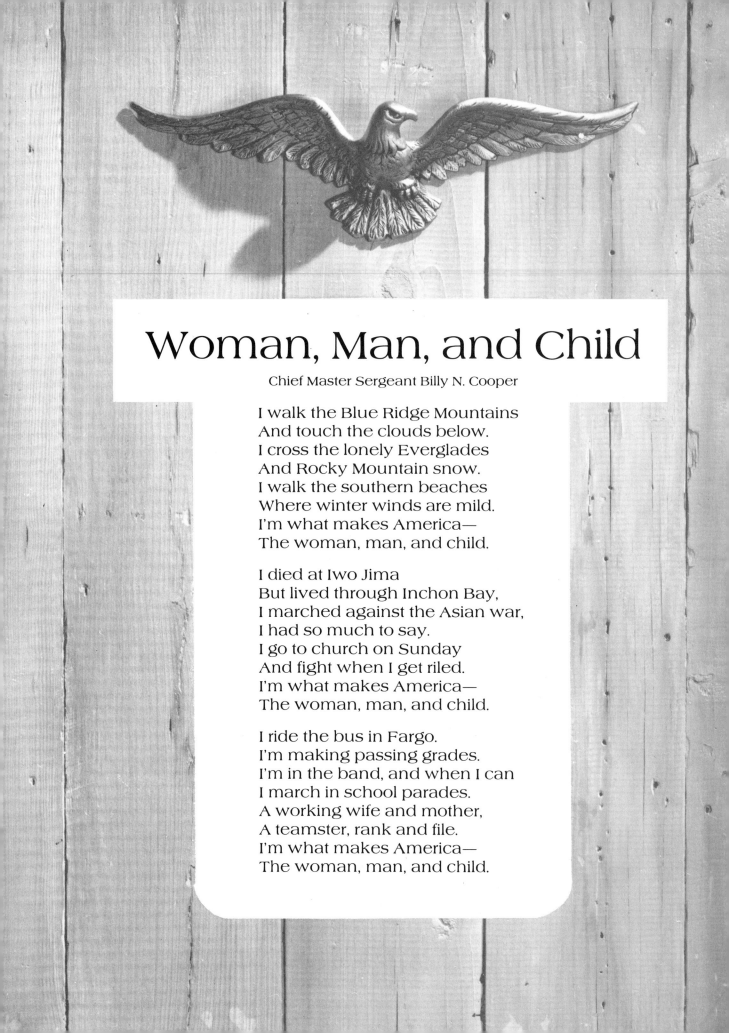

Woman, Man, and Child

Chief Master Sergeant Billy N. Cooper

I walk the Blue Ridge Mountains
And touch the clouds below.
I cross the lonely Everglades
And Rocky Mountain snow.
I walk the southern beaches
Where winter winds are mild.
I'm what makes America—
The woman, man, and child.

I died at Iwo Jima
But lived through Inchon Bay,
I marched against the Asian war,
I had so much to say.
I go to church on Sunday
And fight when I get riled.
I'm what makes America—
The woman, man, and child.

I ride the bus in Fargo.
I'm making passing grades.
I'm in the band, and when I can
I march in school parades.
A working wife and mother,
A teamster, rank and file.
I'm what makes America—
The woman, man, and child.

I load the boats in Memphis
And navigate the stream.
I left New York for Hollywood
But never found my dream.
I shovel snow in Idaho,
Build bridges by the mile.
I'm what makes America—
The woman, man, and child.

A graduate from Harvard,
A dropout from St. Paul,
I fish the southern waters.
I guess I've done it all.
I ask for only justice,
No sentence without trial.
I'm what makes America—
The woman, man, and child.

I live and die, but always try,
My many legends true.
I always stand and take command
Or blame for what I do.
My name is Crockett, Washington,
Lincoln, Lee compiled.
I'm what makes America—
The woman, man, and child.

Salute to the Statue of Liberty

Viney Wilder Endicott

Above the Harbor's busy thoroughfare,
Her right arm lifts a torch for all to see,
Her left hand holds a symbol to declare
That, under God, we all may here be free.

In friendship and goodwill she was conceived
By those who cherished freedom for their own,
Whose fathers died for that which they believed,
Who in the face of tyranny had sown
The seeds that gave the common man new birth,
And clothed him in the cloth of dignity,
Those seeds whose roots had fertilized our earth
And first made green the leaves of liberty.

God help us keep this torch of freedom bright
Above the troubled waters of our time,
That they who walk in darkness shall have light,
And peace may still reward our upward climb.

Not like the brazen giant of Greek fame,
With conquering limbs astride from land to land;
Here at our sea-washed, sunset gates shall stand
A mighty woman with a torch, whose flame
Is the imprisoned lightning, and her name
Mother of Exiles. From her beacon-hand
Glows world-wide welcome; her mild eyes command
The air-bridged harbor that twin cities frame.
"Keep, ancient lands, your storied pomp!" cries she
With silent lips. "Give me your tired, your poor,
Your huddled masses yearning to breathe free,
The wretched refuse of your teeming shore.
Send these, the homeless, tempest-tost to me,
I lift my lamp beside the golden door!"

Inscription on the Statue of Liberty
Emma Lazarus, 1883

I Hear America Singing

Walt Whitman

I hear America singing, the varied carols I hear,
Those of mechanics, each one singing his as it should be
    blithe and strong,
The carpenter singing his as he measures his plank or
    beam,
The mason singing his as he makes ready for work or
    leaves off work,
The boatman singing what belongs to him in his boat, the
    deckhand singing on the steamboat deck,
The shoemaker singing as he sits on his bench, the hatter
    singing as he stands,
The woodcutter's song, the plowboy's on his way in the
    morning, or at noon intermission or at sundown,
The delicious singing of the mother, or of the young wife at
    work, of the girl sewing or washing,
Each singing what belongs to him or her and to none else,
The day what belongs to the day—at night the party of
    young fellows, robust, friendly,
Singing with open mouths their strong melodious songs.

The Republic

Henry Wadsworth Longfellow

Thou, too, sail on, O Ship of State!
Sail on, O Union, strong and great!
Humanity with all its fears,
With all the hopes of future years,
Is hanging breathless on thy fate!
We know what Master laid thy keel,
What workmen wrought thy ribs of steel,
Who made each mast, and sail, and rope,
What anvils rang, what hammers beat,
In what a forge and what a heat
Were shaped the anchors of thy hope!
Fear not each sudden sound and shock;
'Tis of the wave and not the rock;
'Tis but the flapping of the sail,
And not a rent made by the gale!
In spite of rock and tempest's roar,
In spite of false lights on the shore,
Sail on, nor fear to breast the sea!
Our hearts, our hopes, are all with thee,
Our hearts, our hopes, our prayers, our tears,
Our faith triumphant o'er our fears,
Are all with thee—are all with thee!

Daughters of America

William Lightfoot Visscher

Ring out, ye bells, your sweetest chimes;
Sing, all ye poets, dulcet rhymes;
Shout loud, ye crowds, in strongest praise;
Shine out, fair sun, in softest rays.
    And dance, ye rippling waters.
For Freedom's sons will sing a song,
That in a chorus, high and strong,
Shall sounding ring, from sea to sea,
Whose grandest harmony shall be,
    America's true daughters.

Oh, they are loyal, brave and true,
And fair the red, and white and blue,
That in the nation's colors rise,
Shine in their cheeks and brows and eyes
    And glow upon their banners.
From ocean shore to mountain crest;
From north and south and east and west;
From all the bright and beauteous land,
They come, a blessing-laden band,
    And singing sweet hosannahs.

With cheering words from such a mouth
As thine, oh daughter of the south!
And love from such a loyal breast
As thine, oh daughter of the west!
    The sons can never falter.
And while in north and east shall stand
The loyal, helping, sister band,
Sweet Freedom's day shall know no night,
But ever shall the flame glow bright
    Upon the country's altar.

The Parade

Richmond George Anthony

The parade! The parade!
We mustn't miss the parade!
The soldiers will march for half of the
    town,
Their arms swinging smartly, up and
    then down,
With rifles slung over shoulders of
    brown.
    Sandra, have you
    Tied the lace in your shoe?
    We mustn't miss the parade!

The parade! The parade!
We mustn't miss the parade!
The bands will be there. A
    rooty-toot-toot.
Who doesn't love drums, the sound
    of a flute?
And then there's the tall drum major,
    to boot.
    Shelley, make haste—
    Not a moment to waste!
    We mustn't miss the parade!

The parade! The parade!
We mustn't miss the parade!
The guard with the flags will proudly
    step by
And off will come Daddy's hat. You
    and I
Will cheer as the colors wave for our
    eye.
    Is Sandra with us?
    Climb into the bus.
    We mustn't miss the parade!

The parade! The parade!
We mustn't miss the parade!
The lodges will have their drill teams,
    of course.
The Boy and the Girl Scouts will be
    out in full force,
All led by the marshall on a white
    horse.
    Take Shelley's hand.
    I hear a band.
    We mustn't miss the parade!

Fourth of July

Earle J. Grant

Our country is festive
When the Fourth of July comes,
With the blare of bugles
And the roll of drums . . .

In its mountain setting
Of verdant green,
Our small town is a part
Of the joyous scene.

Activities are planned
For everyone,
And all are invited
To join in the fun.

Fireworks appear
To blossom in the night
In red, white, and blue—
A thrilling sight.

We praise our God
Who blesses our nation
As, alive and free,
We join the celebration!

Photo Overleaf
COAST OF OREGON
George Schwartz

HARGREAVES 76

Gather Rose Petals
to Preserve Summer Scents

Carole McCray

In an herb garden, there is more than meets the eye. The leaves of the herb plants contain strongly scented oils, released either by the sun's warmth or by the simple rubbing of leaves between your fingertips. Also, after an unexpected soft rainshower on a steaming humid day, you find a sweetness of fragrances in the herb garden.

Helen Keller spoke of such unseen sweet scents in her statement, "I doubt if there is any sensation arising from sight more delightful than the odors which filter through sun-warmed, wind-tossed branches on the tide of scents which swells, subsides, rises again on wave after wave, filling the wide world with invisible sweetness."

I am reminded of her words after a summer rain. A downpour suddenly drenches our plants; it passes quickly, and within an hour the sun is shining. Or a gentle showering from the sky will last several hours, and the heavy humidity of the summer's day returns. Such times are perfect for experiencing the aroma of herbal plants. Spearmint, peppermint, orange, and pineapple are more pungent than ever. The peppery fragrance of the bushy oregano along with the sweet basil's spicy scents fill the hot air. Walking near the lemon thyme, I catch a whiff of citrus from the golden plant.

The olfactory pleasures derived from herbs can sometimes ease the cares of a frenzied day, and a world-weary spirit may be soothed amidst the relaxing experience of an herbal garden. In the quiet of the early morning, I delight in gathering rose-scented geranium leaves used in making potpourri. The strong scent of roses permeates the air as I pick the leaves and place them in my basket.

The best time for collecting leaves, garden flowers, or any of the colorful wildflowers to dry is early in the day, between 8:00 and 10:00 a.m., on a sunny day at least one to two days after it has rained. Whatever is gathered for drying should be placed on a drying screen in an airy, sunless room. I made a drying screen from window screening. Cheesecloth can also be used. Two or three layers of cheesecloth or a single layer of window screening tautly attached to a rectangular-shaped wooden frame makes a very good drying rack.

Spread the leaves, petals, and flowers on the rack, allowing air to circulate around them until they are as dry as cornflakes. This process usually takes about two weeks, but the gathering can continue all summer. Once the potpourri is made, store it in an airtight container in a dark place, allowing six weeks for the mixture to mellow. You are then ready to transfer it into jars for gift giving.

Your potpourri is a very personal statement, for you can experiment with flowers, herbs, and spices from your garden and kitchen. Your sense of smell will guide you. To capture the essence of summer, here is a recipe for a do-it-yourself potpourri:

Rose Potpourri

2 quarts mixed red and pink rose petals
1 handful of rosemary leaves
4 tablespoons ground orris root (may be obtained from a pharmacy or herb shop; it is a fixative to retain fragrances)
5 drops oil (vetiver, santal, or rose oil)
1 pint lemon verbena leaves
1 tablespoon grated orange peel
4 tablespoons mixed crushed spices (cinnamon, ginger, clove, nutmeg)

Dry the rose petals, lemon verbena leaves, and rosemary leaves. Place rose petals, verbena, and rosemary leaves in large mixing bowl; toss lightly. Blend the orange peel with orris root and crushed spices. Mix with the contents of mixing bowl. Add drops of oil and place in airtight container for mellowing period, about six weeks. Your potpourri is ready to transfer into jars or bottles, or you may wish to have it remain in the larger container until you are ready to transfer it to smaller glass jars or decorative tins for freshening a room. An occasional shaking or stirring will heighten the scent. If the fragrance begins to fade, just add a drop of the oil to revive the potpourri. The scent of summer will be yours, preserved and bottled now to freshen stark winter days.

Reach Your Hand to Me

James Whitcomb Riley

Reach your hand to me, my friend,
  With its heartiest caress—
Sometime there will come an end
  To its present faithfulness—
    Sometime I may ask in vain
    For the touch of it again,
    When between us land or sea
    Holds it ever back from me.

Sometime I may need it so,
  Groping somewhere in the night,
It will seem to me as though
  Just a touch, however light,
    Would make all the darkness day,
    And along some sunny way
    Lead me through an April shower
    Of my tears to this fair hour.

Oh, the present is too sweet
  To go on forever thus!
Round the corner of the street
  Who can say what waits for us?—
    Meeting—greeting, night and day,
    Faring each the selfsame way—
    Still somewhere the path must end—
    Reach your hand to me, my friend!

Photo Opposite
TO KEEP IN TOUCH
Fred Sieb

Good humor makes all
things tolerable.

Henry Ward Beecher

Talking with a friend is
nothing but thinking
aloud.

Addison

Be slow in choosing a
friend, slower in
changing.

Benjamin Franklin

All green and fair
summer lies, just
budded from the b[...]
of spring.

Susan Cool[...]

Of friends, however
humble, scorn not one.

Wordsworth

A *true friend is one soul in two bodies.*

Aristotle

No star is ever lost we once have seen,
We always may be what we might have been.

Adelaide A. Procter

Nature, like man, sometimes weeps for gladness.

Disraeli

e swallow alone does make the summer.

Cervantes

Oh, the summer night has a smile of light And she sits on a sapphire throne.

B.W. Procter

Country Chronicle

Lansing Christman

Those inviting entrances to old country homes were called verandas when I was growing up on the farm. I always thought of ours as a restful retreat.

As a child, I sought a brief siesta behind the latticed posts of the veranda before returning to the fields after the summer noonday meal. Resting and dreaming there, I would listen to fledgling orioles chirping from pouch-like nests in the elms. Cicadas rasped their vibrating chords high in the trees.

In the evening hours, the veranda was a haven to which the whole family turned. We waited for the change from dusk to darkness. We cherished the cricket tremolo, the organ roll of the thrush, the whippoorwill's call. We sat long after twilight watching fireflies flash their incandescent lights in their flights above the grass dampened by dew.

The veranda was shelter from thundershowers and refreshing rains. Wicker chairs creaked as we sat and rocked to the accompaniment of pattering rain on roof and leaf. It was both comforting and invigorating.

Summer weekends on the farm lured friends from the city to share the peace and serenity of the hills. They gathered on Sunday afternoons on the open porch, sipping lemonade, or relishing homemade ice cream dipped from a hand-cranked wooden churn.

Today as well, and all year long, a veranda can be a stepping stone to an enduring kinship with the world outside the door. It can be a window to autumn's brilliant hues, to winter lanes submerged in snow. It can be a window to spring's first warming rays. Now it is a doorway to June's maturing gardens and to fields with meadow melodies.

Friendship's Opportunity

Hilda Sanderson

Was it to keep me out, I mused,
This fence of privacy—
The one my neighbor had put up
So independently?

Oh, it was nice, a trellis style
Sprayed with a cedar stain,
But did it mean those backyard chats
We'd never have again?

With feelings somewhat injured,
I examined it once more,
And found within that trellised wall
A swinging, unlatched door.

And as I pushed it open
My neighbor stepped right through,
And said of her old yard dog,
"Now he can't bother you."

"I've worried and I've worried,"
She went on to explain,
"That since he's such a bother,
Our friendship he might strain."

And when we'd talked it over
There was no further doubt,
That neither dogs nor fences
Could keep our friendship out.

For neighbors are as children
Who share a common place—
This friendship's opportunity
Should never go to waste.

A Mile With Me

Henry van Dyke

Oh, who will walk a mile with me
    Along life's merry way?
A comrade blithe and full of glee,
Who dares to laugh out loud and free,
And let his frolic fancy play
Like a happy child, through the flowers gay
That fill the field and fringe the way
    Where he walks a mile with me.

And who will walk a mile with me
    Along life's weary way?
A friend whose heart has eyes to see
The stars shine out o'er the darkening lea,
And the quiet rest at the end o' the day—
A friend who knows, and dares to say
The brave, sweet words that cheer the way
    Where he walks a mile with me.

With such a comrade, such a friend,
I fain would walk till journey's end,
Through summer sunshine, winter rain,
And then?—Farewell, we shall meet again!

Life may scatter us and keep us apart; it may prevent us from thinking very often of one another; but we know that our comrades are somewhere "out there"—where, one can hardly say—silent, forgotten, but deeply faithful. And when our paths cross theirs, they greet us with such manifest joy, shake us so gaily by the shoulders! Indeed, we are accustomed to waiting . . . .

We forget that there is no hope of joy except in human relations. If I summon up those memories that have left with me an enduring savor, if I draw up the balance sheet of the hours in my life that have truly counted, surely I find only those that no wealth could have procured me. True riches cannot be bought. One cannot buy the friendship of a Mermoz, of a companion to

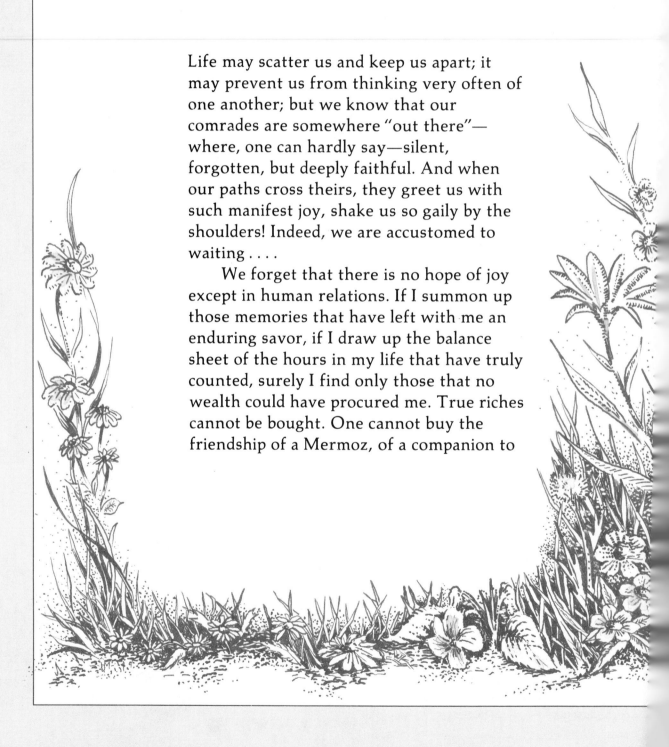

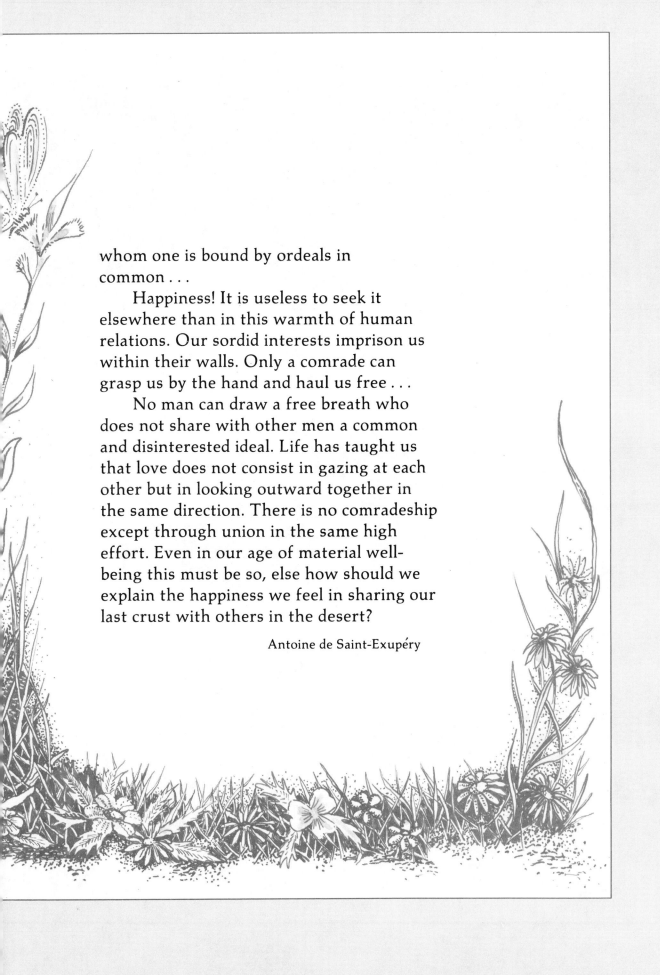

whom one is bound by ordeals in
common . . .

Happiness! It is useless to seek it
elsewhere than in this warmth of human
relations. Our sordid interests imprison us
within their walls. Only a comrade can
grasp us by the hand and haul us free . . .

No man can draw a free breath who
does not share with other men a common
and disinterested ideal. Life has taught us
that love does not consist in gazing at each
other but in looking outward together in
the same direction. There is no comradeship
except through union in the same high
effort. Even in our age of material well-
being this must be so, else how should we
explain the happiness we feel in sharing our
last crust with others in the desert?

Antoine de Saint-Exupéry

On Being a Child

Linda C. Grazulis

There's nothing that matches being a child
With laughter so jolly, so winsome and free,
To dance on the air and swoop like eaglets,
Auditioning for all the world to see;

To gather your toys and play, play, play,
Amused till the sun goes to sleep for the night;
To awaken once more to an early morn
In lush green fields with a wind-happy kite;

Going to Grandma's for dinner—a treat
Sniffing aromas near the screen door;
Home-churned ice cream and old-fashioned taffy
Keep you smiling and yearning for more;

Clinging to Grandpa's gnarled old hand
With nothing but trust so innocent and sweet;
Skipping rope and hiking along
'Cause every day's an adventuresome treat!

Cameos, ballet shoes, a golden halo,
Perhaps a tattered Raggedy Ann;
Metal trucks, sea shells, castles,
Time for frolic in warm summer sand!

It's fun to reminisce about childhood days
When life was free of grown-up cares;
Sometimes I peep through the nursery door
And dream of my own teddy bear.

A Slice of Life

Edgar A. Guest

There goes a boy and his dog right at his heels. Whenever I see that combination, I always think that there is a friendship that selfishness cannot spoil.

In this life we make friends of which we are fortunate to keep a few to the end of the journey. Some are taken from us and some disappoint us. Some find other people with whom they would rather be. But the dog has no idea of selfishness and no knowledge of pride or ambition. That dog would rather be with that boy right now than with the King of England. Millionaires and the leaders of society, the so-called great of the city could be passing by and that dog wouldn't even turn to look. They might whistle or call to him and he wouldn't respond. So far as that dog is concerned, the finest human being on earth is that boy master of his. He waits for him to come from school and no matter how poorly he might have spelled or how indifferent his work may have been, that dog will be glad to see him when he returns.

It is so when we are grown up. In spite of all our shortcomings, the dog sees in us only the good. Bankrupts may come home, but the dogs will wag their tails to greet them. Sometimes I think it is too bad that we allow our friendships to be spoiled by the temporary failures and disappointments and defeats.

A boy and his dog make a glorious pair:
No better friendship is found anywhere,
For they talk and they walk and they run
   and they play,
And they have their deep secrets for many
   a day;
And that boy has a comrade who thinks
   and who feels,
Who walks down the road with a dog at
   his heels.

He may go where he will and his dog will
   be there,
May revel in mud and his dog will not care;
Faithful he'll stay for the slightest command

And bark with delight at the touch of his hand;
Oh, he owns a treasure which nobody steals,
Who walks down the road with a dog at
   his heels.

No other can lure him away from his side;
He's proof against riches and station and pride;
Fine dress does not charm him, and flattery's
   breath
Is lost on the dog, for he's faithful to death;
He sees the great soul which the body
   conceals—
Oh, it's great to be young with a dog at
   your heels!

Where Shall We Land?

James Whitcomb Riley

All listlessly we float
Out seaward in the boat
　That beareth Love.
Our sails of purest snow
Bend to the blue below
　And to the blue above.
　　Where shall we land?

We drift upon a tide
Shoreless on every side,
　Save where the eye
Of Fancy sweeps far lands
Shelved slopingly with sands
　Of gold and porphyry.
　　Where shall we land?

The fairy isles we see,
Loom up so mistily—
　So vaguely fair,
We do not care to break
Fresh bubbles in our wake
　To bend our course for there.
　　Where shall we land?

The warm winds of the deep
Have lulled our sails to sleep,
　And so we glide
Careless of wave or wind,
Or change of any kind,
　Or turn of any tide.
　　Where shall we land?

We droop our dreamy eyes
Where our reflection lies
　Steeped in the sea,
And, in an endless fit
Of languor, smile on it
　And its sweet mimicry.
　　Where shall we land?

"Where shall we land?" God's grace!
I know not any place
　So fair as this—
Swung here between the blue
Of sea and sky, with you
　To ask me, with a kiss,
　　"Where shall we land?"

Tranquility

Gertrude Williams Siesholtz

I walk alone beside the waters,
   A sea gull soars above the foam,
Tiny sailboats drift along slowly—
   What a peaceful place to roam.

Stately trees stand secluded
   Beneath clouds that dot an azure sky;
Bronze-coated stone forms boundaries
   Where soft-crested waves with spray mount high.

So much beauty to behold
   From a casual stroll beside the sea;
My soul overflows with quiet rapture,
   Blessed with complete tranquility.

I pause awhile to ponder it all,
   Then as I slowly onward trod,
My heart is filled with knowing wonder
   Viewing such perfect gifts of God.

Alone by the Sea

Clare Curley

I love the sea; its lonely haunts
　　Of windswept, sandy dunes
Tower above the roaring waves
　　And reach up for the moon.

The hoary surf comes rolling in
　　And scatters all its gems
Of pearly, luminescent shells—
　　A mermaid's diadem.

The waves are silvered by the stars;
　　The sea in stillness lies,
Reflecting, like a sheet of ice,
　　The deep cerulean skies.

I wander by the shore at night
　　And watch the crested waves,
Because the sea is lonely, too,
　　But she is calm and brave.

COLLECTOR'S CORNER

Countless people the world over have discovered the magic of deltiology (del-tee-AH-logee). Some of them have been deltiologists for years and didn't know it.

Deltiology is the art of collecting picture postcards, according to the *Oxford English Dictionary*. Collecting picture postcards started around the turn of the century and has gained in favor and respect with collectors everywhere.

The history of deltiology begins over a hundred years ago. The U.S. government printed the first postals, or postcards, in 1873. In that same year, private publishers began printing illustrations on commercial postcards. It was not until the 1894 Columbian Exhibition in Chicago that such cards were widely sold as souvenirs. Before 1898, these mailing pieces required full letter-rate postage, two cents at the time, rather than the one-cent rate of government postals. On May 19, 1898, Congress passed the Private Mailing Card Act that permitted privately-printed cards to be mailed at the postal card rate. This opened the floodgates, and picture postcards became the rage.

From the turn of the century, vacationers could expect to find postcard views as they visited New York, Boston, San Francisco, and other major cities. Postcards were prominent at resorts and inns and tourist attractions. Souvenir postcards sent from Coney Island, Atlantic City, and Niagara Falls proved to be cheerful greetings and conversation pieces in American homes during the years of Teddy Roosevelt and William Taft. Families took pride in their postcard albums featuring wide varieties of cards mailed from different places around the world. Before the days of radio and television, these albums were a major source of entertainment and pleasure.

During the golden age of the postcard, 1905-1913, the picture postcard was everywhere. Mail carriers were loaded with them, especially before holidays such as New Year's Day, Valentine's Day, Easter, Thanksgiving, and Christmas. Cards were also available for Lincoln's and Washington's birthday celebrations, Mother's Day, and Halloween. And, of course, for birthdays. Get-well cards appeared at this time. One could not walk down Main Street without seeing cards for sale in store windows and on sidewalk racks. Salesmen wearing display racks walked the streets hacking postcards at bargain prices.

Holiday and personal greetings were not the only cards that flowed during the golden age. Publishers, large and small, produced views of streets, trolleys, parks, lakes, rivers, bridges, schools, churches, banks, post offices, and nearly every conceivable topographical image. Souvenir cards were available for World's Fairs and local events. Merchants and manufacturers sent postcards to advertise their products. Theaters and entertainers mailed them to promote their shows. Churches sent postcards to announce services or to remind a Sunday school student of a recent absence. Publishers printed and distributed humorous cards. Others published cards in sets such as the presidents, state capitols, the Ten Commandments, Indians, famous paintings, ships, animals, and hundreds of other subjects. Connoisseurs in other collecting fields, in fact, have found deltiology a natural supplement to their primary interests.

Not only have postcards depicted almost every known subject, but they have been produced in a wide variety of ways including lithography, embossing, engraving, and screening. Postcard production during the golden age included cards made of aluminum, copper, wood, celluloid, leather, and other imaginative materials. Producers seemed to rush to be first to add something new to postcards to make them more elaborate such as ribbons, feathers, buttons, glass eyes, pin cushions, mother-of-pearl, tinsel, metal objects, real hair, dried flowers, calendar pads, and even pieces of corn to make what is sometimes called a "corn face" postcard. The most desirable cards now are choice pioneer views printed before 1898, particular artist-signed greetings, and detailed views of small-town Main Streets.

When picture postcards first appeared, collectors considered them a passing fancy. However, that attitude has shifted through the years. Today deltiologists are found everywhere. Thousands have joined local and international clubs, many have spent considerable time and resources on their collections, and hundreds have attended postcard exhibitions to get to know other collectors.

Perhaps you will soon be among the ranks of those who have found these fascinating pieces of art and social history a magic carpet into a new and delightful world. You may even be a deltiologist and didn't know it.

James Lewis Lowe

Heart of the Woods

Margaret E. Sangster

Such beautiful things in the heart of the woods!
  Flowers and ferns, and the soft green moss;
Such love of the birds, in the solitudes,
  Where the swift winds glance, and the treetops toss;
Spaces of silence, swept with song,
  Which nobody hears but the God above;
Spaces where myriad creatures throng,
  Sunning themselves in his guarding love.

Such safety and peace in the heart of the woods,
  Far from the city's dust and din,
Where passion nor hate of man intrudes,
  Nor fashion nor folly has entered in.
Deeper than hunter's trail hath gone
  Glimmers the tarn where the wild deer drink;
And fearless and free comes the gentle fawn,
  To peep at herself o'er the grassy brink.

Such pledges of love in the heart of the woods!
  For the Maker of all things keeps the least,
And over the tiny floweret broods,
  With care that for ages has never ceased.
If he cares for this, will he not for thee—
  Thee, wherever thou art today?
Child of an Infinite Father, see—
  And safe in such gentlest keeping stay.

Vacation Land

Eleanor Fiock

Last night I slept beneath the friendly pines,
Beneath a canopy of leafy lace
    Held high above my head.
While pillowed on the cool, sweet-scented earth,
Whose certain fragrance seemed to fill the place,
This heart of mine was touched to reverent flame;
And high above, a slowly rising moon
    Dropped moonbeams on my bed.

I think the angels surely soar abroad,
Their airy wings spread magic as they pass
    On their nocturnal flight.
The purple dome ablaze with stellar orbs
Reveals the quivering diamonds in the grass.
Like some colossal handiwork of God,
The sombre mountains rise, majestic, tall . . .
    An awe-inspiring sight.

Oh, such a night of dreams and sweet content,
With beauty spilling over stream and hill
    Adorning tree and sod.
While lying in that pale celestial light
With naught to do but dream and drink my fill
From nature's beauty cup so richly blent,
I knew that sometime—'twixt dusk and dawn—
    All earth communed with God.

The Lighthouse

Henry Wadsworth Longfellow

The rocky ledge runs far into the sea,
    And on its outer point, some miles away,
The Lighthouse lifts its massive masonry,
    A pillar of fire by night, of cloud by day.

Even at this distance I can see the tides,
    Upheaving, break unheard along its base,
A speechless wrath, that rises and subsides
    In the white lip and tremor of the face.

And as the evening darkens, lo! how bright,
    Through the deep purple of the twilight air,
Beams forth the sudden radiance of its light
    With strange, unearthly splendor in its glare!

Not one alone; from each projecting cape
    And perilous reef, along the ocean's verge,
Starts into life a dim, gigantic shape,
    Holding its lantern o'er the restless surge.

Like the great giant Christopher it stands
    Upon the brink of the tempestuous wave,
Wading far out among the rocks and sands,
    The night-o'ertaken mariner to save.

Summer Vacation

Pamela Kennedy

As summer approaches, wanderlust rises in me like sap in the trees, and I long for summer vacation. As a child, I saw summer vacation as freedom from school and the familiar horizons of home. It began with winter evenings spent around the kitchen table when my family poured over maps, picture postcards, and travel brochures: "Camp Mineha-ha, nestled deep in the fragrant, pine-scented woods of Upper Butte, surrounded by native flora and fauna will give your family time to become renewed and refreshed while communing with nature in its natural state." By June each year, we were ready.

The distance from home to our destination wasn't measured in miles, but in how many choruses of "She'll Be Coming round the Mountain" Dad could stand before he got mad. I always punctuated the trips with bouts of car sickness, but getting there was not the point: *being there* was.

Our vacations usually involved camping, and I still recall the scents of wet canvas and pine needles and the roar of rushing water. We'd drag armloads of driftwood to the fire ring and pile the wood high for our evening bonfire. We'd toast marshmallows over the glowing coals until they caught fire, then blow them out and squish them between honey grahams layered with chunks of chocolate. The black ashes and white goo made a sticky mess of fingers and faces, but nothing tasted better—ever.

Hygiene took a vacation when we did. The children were *supposed* to get dirty. That proved we were having a good time!

Mother insisted we still do chores, however. I remember washing dishes with a bar of Ivory soap in an enamel basin filled with tepid water. The Ivory left a film on the plates and gave a mild soapy flavor to all our food. We would have hated it at home, but it was the taste of vacation and no one complained.

We camped simply: a tent, a Coleman stove and lantern, and sleeping bags lined with red plaid flannel. For dinner we fixed Camper's Stew, baked potatoes wrapped in foil, and hot dogs speared on sticks and wrapped in biscuit dough. Part of every meal was burned to a crisp and part was raw. But it didn't matter. On vacation no one fussed about the little things.

Mother always pointed out details. On a walk through the woods she would spot a spider spinning a web and describe with awe the intricate patterns it created between the fern fronds. She would spy a column of ants and describe their industry, stooping to place a tiny crumb in their path and then watching to see what they would do with it. She taught me to observe the little dramas in life: the struggle of a leaf to navigate the steam, the anger of a robin at the audacity of a blue jay, the scolding of a mother chipmunk with her disobedient babies. I'm sure Mother didn't have a tremendous amount of knowledge about all of this, but her enthusiasm was contagious.

Father was the pragmatist. He made sure the tent poles were in the right place and at the right angles. He showed me how to build a log cabin fire and a tepee fire, extolling the virtues of each. He instructed me in the proper procedure for baiting a fish hook with a wiggly worm—something I never quite mastered, for all the while I was trying to skewer the squirming thing, I kept thinking about Mother describing its family at home in the earth somewhere wondering why it was late for supper! It was probably good that my parents had different approaches to summer vacation. It certainly made for a richer experience.

As those memories well up again this year, I look at my three children huddled around the kitchen table pouring over technicolor brochures describing Disneyland and Sea World. On our way to the Magic Kingdom we will stop to stay in spotlessly clean motels with sparkling blue swimming pools. There will be no smell of damp canvas nor film of Ivory soap on the china. As we navigate the freeways, my pragmatic husband will be

preoccupied with miles per gallon and the shortest distance between two rest stops. I, on the other hand, will point out the little dramas along the way—the clouds racing one another across the sky or, perhaps, two young stallions frolicking in a field. My sons will be singing the fifty-sixth chorus of "John Jacob Jingleheimer Smith," and my daughter will, no doubt, get carsick.

Despite my nostalgia, there is something to be said for meals cooked by someone else and a bed free of beetles. Times have changed, but maybe things aren't so different: families still laugh and argue, love and teach, stretch and grow together. It will be a great summer vacation again this year, and perhaps someday my children will entertain their own families with fond memories of summers past.

Photo Overleaf
MOUNT RAINIER, WASHINGTON
Larry Burton

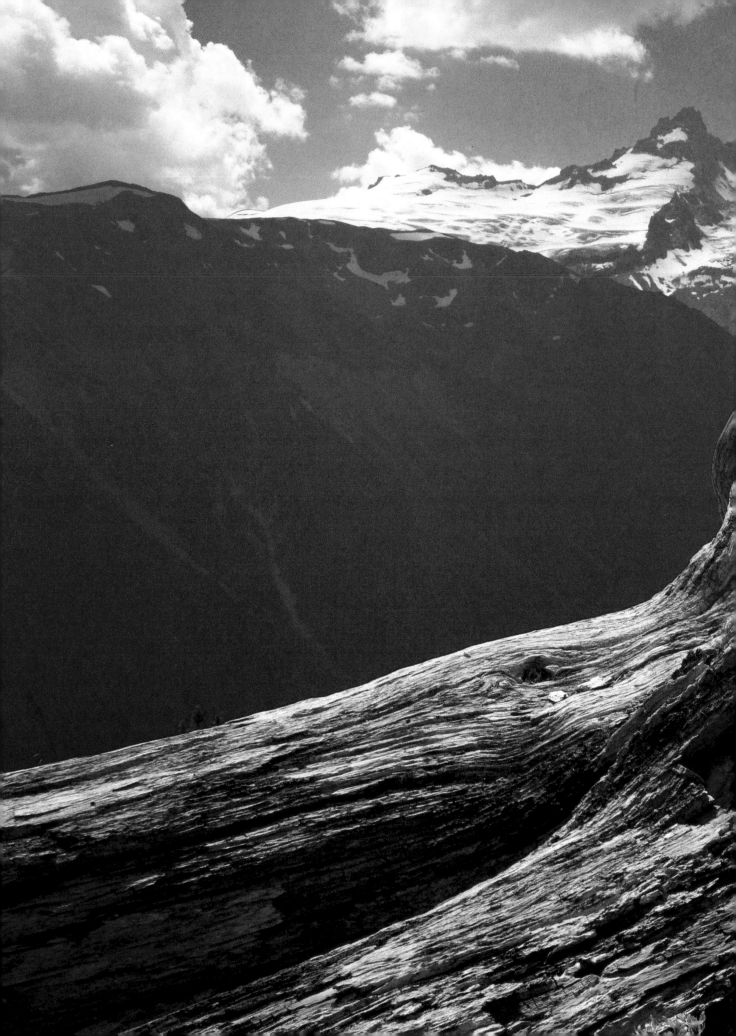

Delightful
Summer Days

Lorice Fiani Mulhern

How delightful are summer days!
Days of golden light and fresh green beauty,
Days of blossom scents and flowers in full
  blooming!

O summer, sweetest season!
Summer of picnics, boating and beaches,
Of perfect freedom while walking or sunning,
And complete relaxing while doing nothing.

O summer, glorious summer!
Days of the sudden, swift shower
  and the clean after-coolness,
Of petals on grass newly scattered,
And skies awash with the mistiest colors.

O summer, summer of soft nights,
Cool dawns and sunsets incomparable!
When the spirit feels the spell
  of the mysterious, the indefinable,
And becomes somehow different, enchanted.

Such is summer, the free and the beautiful,
Like a dream one lives and would not
  abandon.

Think Back to the Good Old Days with I*deals*

Many of us have an old rocking chair resting by a sunny window or on the front porch. There's something comforting about such a rocker. It is one of the good things we have inherited from the past. In our next issue, *Old-Fashioned Ideals*, we celebrate those kinds of things: soda fountains, general stores, country school houses, and more from a time when going out to dinner meant going to a neighbor's house for a meal and card playing.

You will find these themes and more in *Old-Fashioned Ideals*. We look forward to bringing written and visual treats to your home and to the homes of Brenda McCloy, who writes:

> *I just want to tell you how wonderful I think Ideals is. I have gotten the magazine for the last eleven years. I enjoy it so much, and I hope it will continue for many years to come.*

And Nancy Dyson Shipp, who writes:

> *Yesterday I glimpsed a copy of Ideals for the first time. I was struck by the simplicity and beauty of your publication. It's quite remarkable!*

Thank you to Brenda McCloy and Nancy Shipp for your welcome comments.

If you are a regular I*deals* reader, you will love your next issue. And now is a perfect time to introduce a friend to the joys of wonderful poetry, articles, and photography all year long with a subscription—starting with *Old-Fashioned Ideals*.

ACKNOWLEDGMENTS

WOMAN, MAN, AND CHILD by Chief Master Sergeant Billy N. Cooper from *KALEIDO-SCOPE U.S.A.—A POET'S VIEW, VOL. II*, copyright 1987. Used by permission of the author; A BOY AND HIS DOG from *EDGAR A. GUEST BROADCASTING*, copyright 1935, The Reilly & Lee Co. Used by permission; REACH YOUR HAND TO ME and WHERE SHALL WE LAND? from *THE BEST-LOVED POEMS AND BALLADS OF JAMES WHITCOMB RILEY* (Indianapolis: Bobbs-Merrill, 1920); THE PATH THAT LEADS TO NOWHERE by Corinne Roosevelt from *SERVICE AND SACRIFICE*. Copyright 1919 Charles Scribner's Sons; copyright renewed 1947 Corinne Robinson Alsop. Reprinted with the permission of Charles Scribner's Sons, an imprint of Macmillan Publishing Co.; excerpt by Antoine de Saint-Exupery from *WIND, SAND AND STARS*, copyright 1939 by Antoine de Saint-Exupery; renewed 1968 by Harcourt Brace Jovanovich, Inc. Reprinted by permission of the publisher; THEY CALLED IT AMERICA by Rabbi Abba Hillel Silver from *SUNSHINE MAGAZINE*, July, 1966. Used by permission; GRAND CANYON by Sharon Thompson-Dalegowski from *KALEIDOSCOPE U.S.A.—A POET'S VIEW, VOL. II*, copyright 1987. Used by permission of the author; DAUGHTERS OF AMERICA from *BLUE GRASS BALLADS AND OTHER VERSE* by William Lightfoot Visscher, copyright 1900; published by H.M. Caldwell Company, New York & Boston; WHEN FATHER WAS A BOY by Anonymous from *CUB SCOUT & WEBELOS SCOUT PROGRAM HELPS 1985-86*, BOY SCOUTS OF AMERICA. Used by permission. Our sincere thanks to the following whose addresses we were unable to locate: Richard George Anthony for THE PARADE; the estate of Eleanor Fiock for VACATION LAND; the estate of Brian F. King for NOW SUMMER WAVES HER MAGIC WAND....